Cats Are Worthless

R SHERWOOD

ISBN: 1451524072
ISBN-13: 9781451524079
Library of Congress Control Number: 2010904502

Cats are worthless as hunting trophies ...

... as lamps ...

... and perfume atomizers.

Cats use four-letter words ...

... make clumsy flyswatters ...

... you can't box with them ...

... and they are non-absorbent as towels.

Cats cannot be used as balloons ...

... or airsick bags ...

... and they never listen to anyone.

Cats make lousy bras ...

... toilet plungers ...

... fire extinguishers ...

... and no one will like what comes out of this piñata.

Cats do not make good bear traps ...

... swimsuits ...

... skeet ...

... or musical instruments.

Cats are useless for home defense ...

... bidets ...

... dairy cows ...

... and they don't even keep the monster under the bed away.

Cats do not last long as dog toys ...

... they make horrible canteens ...

... and very odd dart boards.

Cats make ridiculous cell phones ...

... weak tow ropes ...

... and you can't even paint with them.

Cats are ineffective staplers ...

... axes ...

... and they make wimpy cage fighters.

Cats make fragile road cones ...

... hideous coffee pots ...

... dangerous guide animals ...

... and they don't really have nine lives.

Cats get into your stuff ...

... they are worthless as stadium cushions ...

... they make lame Frisbees ...

... and they are not sturdy step stools.

Cats are awkward hand puppets ...

... horrible record players ...

... terrible alarm clocks ...

... stupid umbrellas ...

... and they are much too small to be comfortable bean-bag chairs.

Cats do not make good bait ...

... sleds ...

... cigarette lighters ...

... or swimmers.

You can't bowl with a cat ...

... or run with them ...

... they make lumpy book marks ...

... and they are not bullet proof.

You can't play basketball with a cat ...

... they are poor speed bumps ...

... make terrible flint ...

... ridiculous air bags ...

... idiotic ping pong balls ...

... useless hairbrushes ...

... and awful wallets.

Cats make stupid shower caps ...

... crappy tether balls ...

... and lackadaisical rodeo bulls.

Cats are much too full of gristle.

Cats make ridiculous toupees ...

... hood ornaments ...

... clothes lines ...

... and they often forget where their litter box is located.

Cats do not make good parachutes.

Cats make lopsided footballs ...

... and even more lopsided golf balls.

Cats make embarrassing car horns.

Cats do not make good hard hats ...

... car jacks ...

... or water skis ...

... and they don't last long as land mine detectors.

Made in the USA
Las Vegas, NV
01 April 2023

70028265R00046